AF473985

VERMOUTH

A Classic Revival

Contents

THE VERMOUTH DRINKS

1
A Brief History of Vermouth

Picture yourself sitting at a sun-dappled café in Turin, a glass of chilled Vermouth in hand, its complex herbal aroma drifting upward as you sip. This moment could be happening today—or more than two centuries ago. Vermouth, that enigmatic, herbaceous fortified wine, has a story that weaves through ancient empires, royal courts, and smoky cocktail bars.

Ancient Beginnings

The idea of infusing wine with herbs and botanicals is older than Vermouth itself. The Greeks and Romans were doing it thousands of years ago—not for happy hour, but as medicine. Back then, wine was often bittered with wormwood (yes, the same herb that would later define Vermouth) and other botanicals to aid digestion, boost energy, or ward off illness. Think of it as ancient health tonics disguised as something you'd actually want to drink.

But while these early aromatized wines laid the groundwork, the Vermouth we know and love didn't officially come onto the scene until much later—and with much more style.

Turin: The Birthplace of Modern Vermouth

Fast-forward to late 18th-century Italy. The setting: Turin, the capital of the Piedmont region, nestled at the foot of the Alps. In 1786, Antonio Benedetto Carpano, a clever distiller and herbalist, created what's widely regarded as the first

Antonio Benedetto Carpano (1764–1815), the Turin distiller credited with inventing modern vermouth in 1786, blending wine with herbs and spices to create a new aperitif tradition.

"modern" Vermouth. His secret? He sweetened his fortified wine and infused it with a blend of exotic botanicals, prominently featuring wormwood (from the German word *wermut*, which gave Vermouth its name). Carpano's concoction was richer, more complex, and infinitely more palatable than the medicinal wines of antiquity.

Soon enough, Carpano's bar near the Royal Palace became the place for the local elite to gather and sip this stylish new aperitif. From there, Vermouth quickly became part of the social fabric of Italy, entwined with the emerging *aperitivo* culture—those leisurely pre-dinner drinks meant to whet the appetite and slow down the day.

Crossing Borders: France Joins the Party

As word of Vermouth spread across the Alps into France, new styles began to emerge. Where Turin specialized in sweeter, darker versions (what we now call Rosso or sweet Vermouth), the French, particularly around Chambéry and Marseille, began crafting drier, lighter expressions.

French producers like Noilly Prat took inspiration from the Provençal landscape—herbs like chamomile, thyme, and lavender made appearances in their blends. And instead of sweeter concoctions, they leaned into a bone-dry, briny style, perfect for oysters and seafood-heavy aperitifs.

By the mid-19th century, both Italian and French styles were flourishing, each distinct but equally beloved.

Vermouth & the Golden Age of Cocktails

While Vermouth was already a staple at European cafés, its next big act came thanks to the rise of the cocktail in the mid-to-late 1800s—especially in America.

Bartenders in New York, New Orleans, and San Francisco began mixing Vermouth with whiskey, gin, and bitters, creating drinks we still order today: the Manhattan, the Martini, the Negroni. Vermouth's herbal backbone gave these cocktails elegance and balance, tempering the punch of high-proof spirits with subtle sweetness and complexity.

By the early 20th century, Vermouth wasn't just a European aperitif—it was essential to modern cocktail culture.

Prohibition & Vermouth's Slump

Then came Prohibition. In the 1920s, America's love affair with Vermouth hit a brick wall as alcohol was outlawed. While Vermouth could still be found in Europe, the U.S. mar-

Once a staple of bar culture, vermouth was among the most popular aperitifs in the late 19th and early 20th centuries. Bartenders poured it generously—on its own, over ice, or in early cocktails—long before stronger spirits came to dominate the bar scene.

ket largely dried up, and with it, Vermouth's prominent role behind the bar.

Even after Prohibition was repealed, changing tastes and mass production dulled Vermouth's sparkle. The mid-20th century saw overly sweetened or poorly made versions flooding bars and home liquor cabinets, often left to oxidize for months. Vermouth became that dusty bottle in the back, associated with syrupy cocktails or watered-down Martinis.

The Vermouth Renaissance

But like all good things, Vermouth has made a triumphant comeback.

In recent years, bartenders, sommeliers, and adventurous drinkers have rediscovered its charms. Craft producers across the globe are reviving traditional methods—small-batch infusions, local botanicals, and careful aging—giving Vermouth the respect it deserves. From boutique Italian houses making bitter, Alpine-style reds to experimental producers in the U.S. and Australia riffing on tradition, Vermouth is no longer an afterthought. It's center stage again.

And today, whether you're sipping a crisp white Vermouth on a rooftop terrace or stirring up a perfectly balanced Boulevardier, you're part of a living history—a thread connecting the herbal tonics of the ancient world, the glamorous cafés of Turin and Paris, and the creative energy of modern bars.

2

How Vermouth is Made

At first glance, Vermouth might seem like just another bottle of wine. But crack it open, and suddenly you're in a garden, an apothecary, maybe even a forest floor after rain. That's the magic of Vermouth—it's wine, yes, but with layers of botanicals that take your senses on a journey.

So, how exactly does a humble base wine transform into this complex, bittersweet marvel? Let's break it down.

It Starts With Wine

All Vermouth begins with wine—typically a neutral, dry white wine that serves as the blank canvas. This might be Trebbiano from Italy, Clairette from southern France, or Macabeo in Spain. These grapes don't scream for attention on their own, but that's the point: the wine needs to be mellow enough to let the botanicals shine later.

In craft Vermouth, some producers are getting adventurous, using higher-quality base wines or even organic and biodynamic grapes to bring subtle nuance to the final blend. But no matter the source, the base wine sets the stage.

The Fortification Step

Once the wine is ready, it's fortified—meaning a neutral grape spirit or brandy is added to boost the alcohol content. This is key. Fortifying stops fermentation and locks in a bit of sweetness if desired. It also helps the Vermouth stay shelf-stable, since it's designed to sit out for a while once opened (although the fridge is always your best bet).

The level of fortification depends on the style. A dry Vermouth might clock in around 16% ABV, while a sweet Vermouth could go up to 18% or more. This balance of wine and spirit is what gives Vermouth its signature silky body and warming kick.

The Heartbeat: Botanicals

Here's where things get really interesting—and where each Vermouth producer starts writing their own secret recipe.

At the center is wormwood (*Artemisia absinthium*), the defining botanical that gives Vermouth its name (*wermut* in German). Historically prized for its bitterness and medicinal properties, wormwood adds a distinct herbal backbone.

But wormwood is just the beginning. Depending on the producer, Vermouth may include:

* Bittering agents like gentian, cinchona bark, or angelica root
* Citrus peels (lemon, orange, bergamot)
* Sweet spices (cinnamon, vanilla, cardamom, cloves)
* Herbs (rosemary, thyme, chamomile, marjoram)
* Florals (rose petals, elderflower, lavender)
* Wild Alpine botanicals (in the case of some Italian and French producers)

Some Vermouths are heavily spiced and brooding, others fresh and floral. The combinations are endless, and producers often guard their botanical blends like family secrets.

Infusion & Maceration

Once the botanicals are selected, they're either steeped (macerated) in the fortified wine or infused via high-proof spirit, creating what's basically a botanical extract. Some houses use both methods, blending infusions with macerations to achieve the desired complexity.

This stage is all about balance—too much bitterness, and the Vermouth becomes harsh; too many sweet spices, and it loses its lift. Skilled blenders act like perfumers, tasting constantly and adjusting ratios until the flavors sing.

Sweetening the Deal

Depending on the style, Vermouth can be bone-dry, semi-sweet, or lusciously rich. This is where sugar or grape must

Some vermouths are aged in wooden barrels, where slow oxidation and contact with oak deepen color, soften bitterness, and add complex notes of spice, vanilla, and dried fruit.

comes in. Sweet Vermouth (rosso) often contains around 10-15% residual sugar, giving it that velvety texture and caramelized note. Dry Vermouth, on the other hand, is barely sweetened, just enough to round off the bitterness.

Blanc or bianco Vermouths sit somewhere in between—crisp but with a touch of sweetness, often showcasing lighter botanicals like vanilla or citrus blossom.

Spanish Vermuts often lean into sweet-and-bitter territory, playing up caramelized sugars and robust bitter herbs, creating a bold aperitif meant to stand up to tapas.

Aging: Fresh or Matured?

Some Vermouths are bottled fresh after blending, but others are aged in oak barrels, stainless steel tanks, or glass demijohns to marry the flavors. Barrel-aging can add layers of spice, dried fruit, and oxidation—think nutty sherry notes or soft tannins.

Producers like Carpano Antica Formula and Noilly Prat age their Vermouths for months, sometimes years, to coax out deeper flavors.

On the flip side, modern craft Vermouth makers might opt for freshness, bottling soon after blending to preserve bright, vibrant aromatics.

Filtering & Bottling

Once the Vermouth is ready, it's filtered to remove solids from the macerated botanicals (unless the producer wants to leave a bit of texture) and bottled under careful conditions.

Some producers may slightly adjust the wine-spirit ratio before bottling, ensuring each batch hits the right alcohol level, sweetness, and intensity.

It's an Art & a Science

At its core, Vermouth is alchemy—blending wine, spirit, botanicals, and time. It's why two sweet Vermouths from Italy can taste wildly different. One may feel like walking through a pine forest; another might remind you of dark chocolate and orange zest on a winter night.

And that's the beauty of Vermouth. Every sip tells a story of place, tradition, and the hands that crafted it.

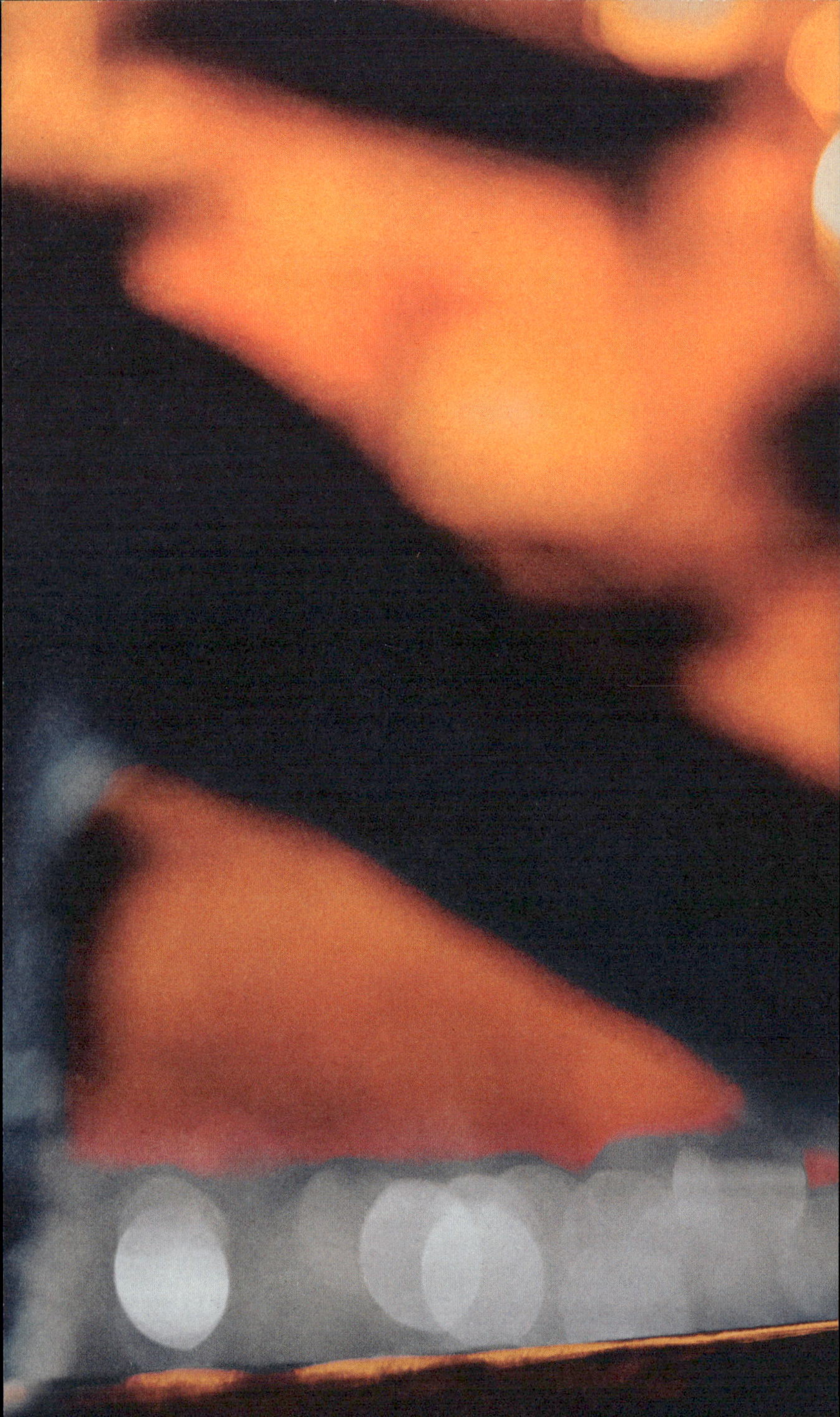

CARPA
CARPA
RPA
Licenza
per la Ditta

3
Vermouth Around the World

Though it may have been born in Turin, Vermouth has since become a global citizen, leaving its aromatic fingerprint on cultures around the world. Each region that makes Vermouth brings its own terroir, traditions, and flair to the glass. Let's take a little tour.

Italy: The Spiritual Home

Italy is where it all began, and to this day, it's the beating heart of Vermouth culture. When people think of classic Vermouth, chances are they're picturing an Italian rosso (sweet red Vermouth).

TURIN & PIEDMONT

Turin is still the mothership. This northern Italian city, with its regal piazzas and old-school cafés, remains synonymous with traditional, sweet Vermouth. Here, rich, complex rosso Vermouths dominate, often layered with baking spices, bitter roots, and Alpine herbs that echo the nearby mountains.

Carpano, Cocchi, and Martini & Rossi are just a few of the big players based in or around Turin, but countless smaller producers are crafting artisanal bottles, many using family recipes passed down for generations.

The Dukes of Savoy helped popularize vermouth in the late 18th century, turning the aromatic fortified wine into a fashionable aperitif at court.

ELSEWHERE IN ITALY

Head south, and you'll find Sicilian Vermouths showcasing Mediterranean botanicals like citrus peel, myrtle, or even local Marsala wines as a base. In Lombardy and other regions, modern producers are creating innovative styles—white, amber, and even rosé Vermouths that nod to both tradition and modern tastes.

The aperitivo ritual is sacred here: picture an early evening, a bustling piazza, a small glass of Vermouth on ice with a lemon peel, and a spread of olives and crisps.

France: Elegance & Restraint

If Italy is bold and warm, French Vermouth is all about subtlety and finesse.

CHAMBÉRY & THE ALPS

Chambéry, nestled in the French Alps, is the only region with protected designation of origin (AOC) status for Vermouth. The standout here is dry Vermouth—think crisp, clean, and lightly herbal.

Dolin is the Chambéry poster child, known for Vermouths that are delicate and refined, with notes of Alpine herbs, citrus, and soft florals. These are the Vermouths that shine in a bone-dry Martini or a classic French aperitif over ice.

Vermuteria La Gloria helped revive Spain's vermouth culture, serving house vermouth on tap with simple tapas and lively neighborhood aperitivo traditions.

RIA
La Gloria
-Desde 2016-

MARSEILLE & PROVENCE

Further south, near Marseille and Provence, you'll find Vermouths kissed by the sun and Mediterranean air. These versions often lean into Provençal herbs like thyme, lavender, and rosemary, alongside citrus peels. The influence of the sea is palpable—there's a slight saline edge that pairs beautifully with seafood and chilled oysters.

French Vermouth tends to be less sweet than its Italian counterparts, making it a favorite for those who enjoy a drier, more herbal profile.

Spain: The Aperitif Renaissance

While Vermouth in Spain (or "Vermut" as they spell it) has always existed, it has exploded back into the limelight thanks to the recent resurgence of *la hora del vermut*—the Vermouth hour.

BARCELONA & MADRID

In cities like Barcelona and Madrid, locals flock to vermuterías—bars dedicated to sipping Vermouth alongside small plates (*tapas*) like anchovies, olives, and cured meats.

Spanish Vermuts tend to have a bolder, more bitter personality, often blending caramelized sweetness with robust botanicals like cardamom, clove, and wormwood. Some even have a slight oxidized quality reminiscent of sherry.

Producers like Yzaguirre, Casa Mariol, and Lustau are leading the charge, making Vermouths that are as perfect for sipping solo as they are for adding punch to a Negroni.

The vibe? Casual, communal, and joyful. In Spain, Vermouth is about slowing down and sharing a moment.

The Rest of Europe: Hidden Gems

SWITZERLAND & AUSTRIA

In the Alps, producers in Switzerland and Austria are creating small-batch Vermouths steeped in mountain herbs, wildflowers, and regional roots like gentian. These versions tend to have a crisp, bracing bitterness, perfect for après-ski moments by the fire.

GERMANY

Germany, with its history of herbal liqueurs and bitters, has a growing number of Vermouth makers blending wormwood with local botanicals and Riesling-based wines. Expect tartness, floral aromatics, and a backbone of bitterness that feels distinctly German.

New-World Vermouths: Innovation & Playfulness

UNITED STATES

Craft distillers in the U.S. have taken Vermouth and run with it, creating wildly inventive styles. From New York's Atsby with its apple-based wines and North American botanicals, to California producers experimenting with organic grapes and unusual herbs, American Vermouth is all about breaking the rules—in a good way.

You'll find everything from bold, red-wine-based Vermouths with a spicy twist to bone-dry white styles with unexpected botanicals like sage, pine, and hops.

AUSTRALIA

Down under, the Australian craft scene is thriving. Vermouth makers here often work with native botanicals—think wattleseed, lemon myrtle, and bush tomato—blended with high-quality Australian wines. Producers like Maidenii are pioneering a distinctively Aussie approach to this European tradition.

SOUTH AMERICA & BEYOND

In Argentina and Chile, Vermouth culture is catching on fast, often drawing influence from Spanish-style Vermuts but using local grapes like Torrontés. Even Japan has begun experimenting with delicate, umami-forward Vermouths incorporating green tea, yuzu, and sansho pepper.

Global Yet Local

What makes Vermouth so fascinating is how adaptable it is. Every region leaves its signature—whether it's the bitter-sweet richness of a Spanish Vermut, the mountain-fresh character of a French Chambéry, or the inventive flair of a Brooklyn distiller.

Yet no matter where it's made, Vermouth carries the same DNA: a wine-based canvas layered with botanicals, culture, and a touch of mystery.

ANTICA FORMULA
Giuseppe B. Carpano
ANTICA RICETTA
VERMOUTH PREGIATO
TEMPUS JUDEX
ANTICA FORMULA
DAL
1786
GIUSEPPE B. CARPANO
PRODOTTO D'ITALIA
Fedele riproduzione
dell'etichetta originale
e della bottiglia
in vetro soffiato.

4
Iconic Vermouth Brands

Walk into a well-stocked liquor store or step behind a bar, and chances are you'll spot some familiar names staring back from the Vermouth shelf. Some of these brands have been around for centuries; others are young upstarts shaking things up. Whether you're sipping it solo or mixing it into a cocktail, these are the bottles that have shaped the world of Vermouth.

Let's meet the legends—and a few modern stars.

The Italian Icons

CARPANO (ANTICA FORMULA)

The O.G. Carpano is the very birthplace of Vermouth as we know it. Created in 1786 in Turin by Antonio Benedetto Carpano, this is the blueprint for sweet, red Vermouth. Its most famous label, Antica Formula, is rich, velvety, and layered with dried fruit, vanilla, cocoa, and baking spice.

Sip it neat over ice, and you're instantly transported to an old-school Italian café. Mix it in a Manhattan or Negroni, and you'll see why bartenders treat it like liquid gold.

MARTINI & ROSSI

Perhaps the most recognizable Vermouth label globally, Martini & Rossi helped put Vermouth in every bar from Milan to Manhattan. Their range covers the bases: Dry, Bianco (a lightly sweet white), and Rosso (their take on sweet Vermouth).

Martini's Dry is classic Martini material—light, herbal, and slightly citrusy. Their Rosso leans approachable and smooth, making it a crowd-pleaser in cocktails.

COCCHI

Cocchi (pronounced "koh-kee") has been crafting Vermouth since 1891, and their Vermouth di Torino is a darling of cocktail enthusiasts. It's a little lighter and fruitier than Antica Formula, with notes of rhubarb, orange peel, and gentle spice. Cocchi's Americano (technically a quinquina) is also a must-try—think of it as a cousin to Lillet, perfect for spritzes.

PUNT E MES

Translating to "point and a half" (a nod to its blend of one point sweetness and half a point bitterness), Punt e Mes is an Italian bartender's secret weapon. It's darker, bolder, and more bitter than many sweet Vermouths—ideal for a Negroni with some extra bite.

A refreshing bittersweet classic made with Punt e Mes, grapefruit juice, and lemon juice, balancing rich vermouth depth with bright citrus and a lively aperitif character.

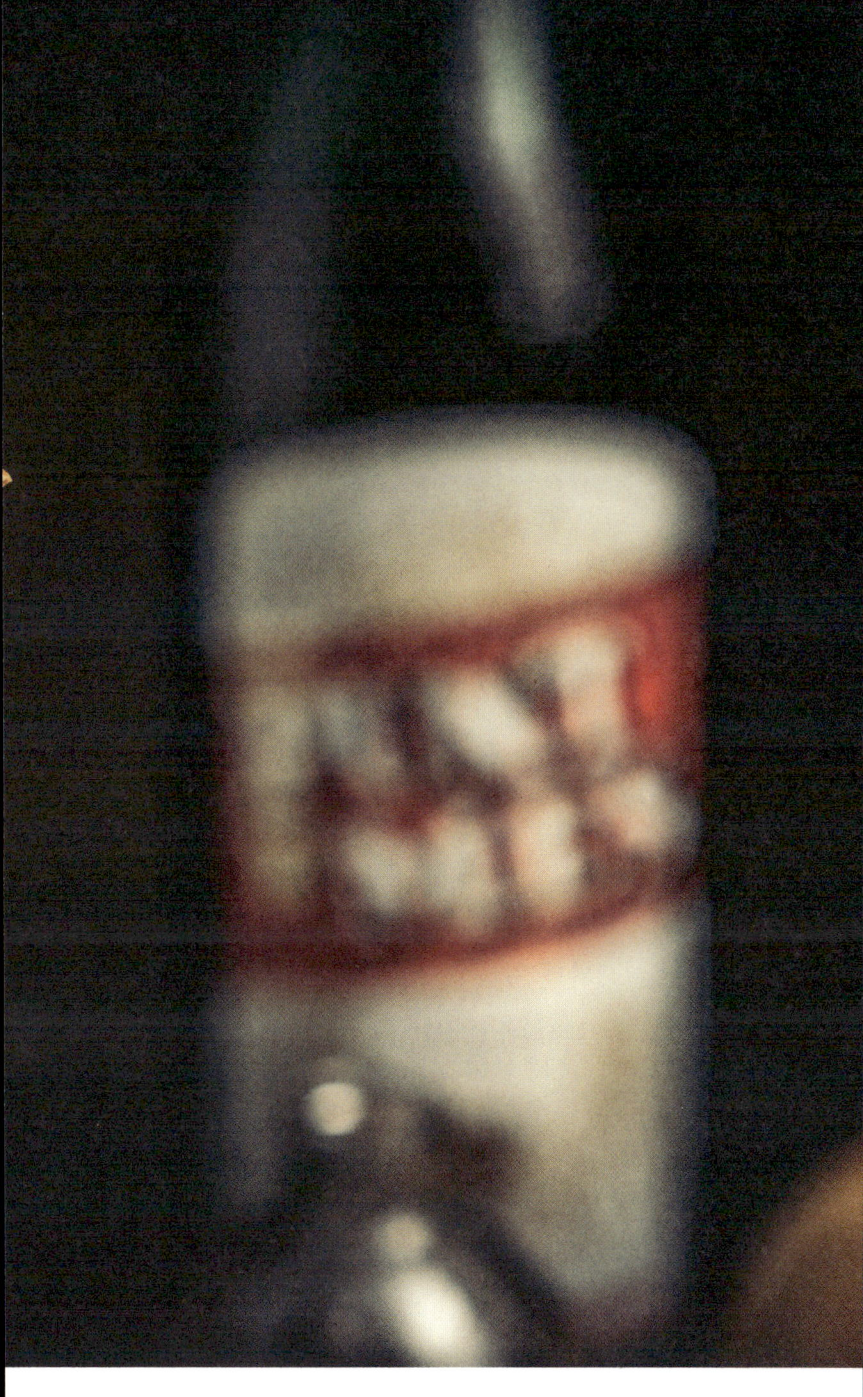

The French Legends

NOILLY PRAT

Hailing from Marseillan, a small town on the French Mediterranean coast, Noilly Prat is the definitive French dry Vermouth. Aged in oak barrels exposed to the salty sea air, this Vermouth is bone-dry, with a savory, briny edge and hints of chamomile, citrus peel, and spice.

It's the go-to for a crisp Martini or simply enjoyed over ice with a twist of lemon.

DOLIN

From the alpine town of Chambéry, Dolin has a history dating back to 1821. Their Vermouths are more delicate and floral compared to their Italian cousins. The Dry version is perfect for lighter cocktails like a classic Martini, while their Blanc (a sweet white Vermouth) shines with notes of vanilla, citrus blossom, and subtle herbs—lovely simply chilled over ice.

Dolin's Vermouth de Chambéry Rouge is also a hidden gem: soft, aromatic, and less bitter than Italian rosso styles.

DRY
DOLIN
Maison fondée en 1821
VERMOUTH
DE
CHAMBÉRY
RHÔNE-ALPES
CRÉATEUR DU VERMOUTH DE CHAMBÉRY – MAISON FONDÉE EN 1821
Louis Ferdinand Dolin
PRODUIT ET MIS EN BOUTEILLE A CHAMBÉRY (FRANCE)

LILLET
1872
Алкогольные напитки 7% и более
ИМПОРТ
LILLET
Maison fondée en 187
PODENSAC - GIRONDE
MADE IN FRANCE
LILLET ROS
17% alc./vol.
A subtle blend of selected wines and fruit
Lillet is made with the greatest care in our
cellars, south of Bordeaux
LILL
Maison fondée
PODENSAC - GIRONDE
MADE IN FRA
LILLET B
17% alc./vol.
A subtle blend of selected wines
Lillet is matured according to
in our Podensac wine cellars
ITALIA
ASTI
AMA

LILLET

Technically a *quinquina* (a wine-based aperitif with quinine), Lillet earns an honorary place here. Produced in Podensac, Bordeaux, Lillet Blanc is a bright, honeyed blend of wine and citrus liqueur. It's famously called for in James Bond's Vesper Martini, but it also makes a sensational spritz or light aperitif.

Lillet also produces a Rosé and a darker, spicier Lillet Rouge, perfect for playing with new cocktail riffs.

The Spanish Staples

YZAGUIRRE

This Catalan Vermouth brand has been around since 1884, producing richly spiced Vermuts that lean sweet and slightly oxidized, with notes of dried fruits, cinnamon, and clove. Their Vermut Rojo Reserva is perfect for sipping with tapas and feels like a warm hug from Barcelona.

LUSTAU

Famed for their sherries, Lustau's Vermut Rojo is a masterpiece. Blending sweet sherry wines like Pedro Ximénez with a complex mix of botanicals, Lustau's Vermouth brings notes of raisins, toffee, nuts, and orange peel. It's decadent but balanced—excellent on its own or in a bold cocktail like a Spanish-style Manhattan.

CASA MARIOL

Casa Mariol crafts a more modern Vermut, often served on tap at Barcelona bars. Their Vermut Negre is dark and bittersweet, with a pronounced herbal edge—perfect with an orange slice and a few anchovy-stuffed olives on the side.

Modern & Craft Producers Worth Knowing

ATSBY (USA)

Based in New York, Atsby is part of the new wave of American Vermouth makers. Using local wines and North American botanicals (apple peel, wild celery seeds, etc.), they're pushing boundaries with complex and inventive takes on classic Vermouth.

MANCINO VERMOUTH (ITALY)

Founded by an Italian bartender, Mancino Vermouth is modern, elegant, and made with an obsessive attention to detail. Their Secco (dry), Bianco Ambrato, and Rosso Amaranto Vermouths have become favorites in high-end cocktail bars.

LA QUINTINYE VERMOUTH ROYAL (FRANCE)

A French standout that marries wine with Cognac and a mix of 28 botanicals. La Quintinye crafts rich, bold Vermouths perfect for those looking for something luxurious and full-flavored, whether in a cocktail or on its own.

La Quintinye
VERMOUTH ROYAL

VERMOUTH
PRODUIT DE
FRANCE
La Quintinye
VERMOUTH ROYAL
ORIGINE CHARENTE
EXTRA
DRY
17% VOL.
750ML.

MAIDENII (AUSTRALIA)

Blending Australian native botanicals like wattleseed and finger lime with French winemaking tradition, Maidenii Vermouths are fresh, innovative, and distinctly Aussie. Their Dry Vermouth, in particular, has found fans in both the cocktail and wine worlds.

So Many Bottles, So Little Time

Whether you're reaching for an Italian rosso for your next Boulevardier or a crisp French dry Vermouth to elevate your Martini, these brands represent the soul of Vermouth's past and present.

And that's the fun part—Vermouth isn't just one thing. It's a category full of surprises, rooted in history but thriving on creativity. Explore a few bottles from different countries, and you'll taste the regional stories in every sip.

MAiDENii
CLASSIC
7
YEAR OLD
VERMOUTH
MAiDENii
CLASSIC
7
YEAR OLD
VERMOUTH
LAND

THE VERMOUTH DRINKS

Dry Martini Cocktail

The Dry Martini is a timeless classic in the cocktail world, celebrated for its simplicity and elegance. It's typically garnished with either an olive or a twist of lemon, adding a subtle touch of flavor. Known for its crisp and clean taste, it's a favorite among many and often considered the quintessential cocktail.

PREP TIME: 5 Mins   YIELD: 1 cocktail

GLASS

Traditionally served in a chilled martini glass.

INGREDIENTS

* 2 1/2 oz (75 ml) gin
* 1/2 oz (15 ml) dry vermouth
* Ice cubes
* Lemon twist or green olive, for garnish

STEP-BY-STEP INSTRUCTIONS

1. Place a martini glass in the freezer for a few minutes or fill it with ice water to chill while you prepare the cocktail.
2. In a mixing glass or a cocktail shaker, combine 2 1/2 ounces of gin and 1/2 ounce of dry vermouth.
3. Fill the mixing glass or shaker with ice cubes.
4. Traditionally, a Dry Martini is stirred, not shaken, to maintain clarity and a silky texture. Use a bar spoon to stir the mixture gently for about 30 seconds. However, if you prefer your Martini shaken, shake it vigorously for about 10 seconds.
5. If you chilled your glass with ice water, empty it now. Strain the Martini mixture into the chilled martini glass using a strainer.
6. Add a garnish of your choice. For a lemon twist, peel a strip of lemon zest, twist it over the drink to release its oils, and drop it in. Alternatively, you can skewer a green olive and place it in the glass.
7. Serve your Dry Martini immediately, enjoying its crisp and aromatic profile.

Negroni Cocktail

The Negroni is a classic Italian cocktail known for its perfectly balanced blend of bitter, sweet, and botanical flavors. It's a simple yet sophisticated drink that's become a staple in cocktail culture around the world.

PREP TIME: 5 Mins YIELD: 1 cocktail

GLASS

Traditionally served in an old-fashioned or rocks glass.

INGREDIENTS

* 1 oz (30 ml) gin
* 1 oz (30 ml) sweet vermouth
* 1 oz (30 ml) Campari
* Ice cubes
* Orange slice or twist, for garnish

STEP-BY-STEP INSTRUCTIONS

1. Start by filling an old-fashioned glass with ice cubes. This will chill the glass and keep your drink cold.
2. Measure out 1 ounce of gin, 1 ounce of sweet vermouth, and 1 ounce of Campari. Pour all three ingredients directly into the glass over the ice.
3. Using a bar spoon, gently stir the mixture for about 20–30 seconds.
4. Cut a fresh slice of orange or peel a strip of orange zest. Gently squeeze the peel over the drink to release its oils, then drop it into the glass as a garnish.
5. Present your Negroni immediately while it's still cold.

Sweet Martini Cocktail

The Sweet Martini is a delightful variation of the classic Martini, featuring a sweeter profile thanks to the use of sweet vermouth. It's a perfect choice for those who enjoy a more rounded and less dry cocktail, while still appreciating the elegance of a Martini.

PREP TIME: 5 Mins YIELD: 1 cocktail

GLASS

Traditionally served in an old-fashioned or rocks glass.

INGREDIENTS

* 2 oz (60 ml) gin
* 1 oz (30 ml) sweet vermouth
* 1 dash of orange bitters (optional)
* Ice cubes
* Maraschino cherry, for garnish

STEP-BY-STEP INSTRUCTIONS

1. Start by chilling your martini glass. You can do this by placing it in the freezer for a few minutes or by filling it with ice water while you prepare the cocktail.
2. In a mixing glass, combine 2 ounces of gin and 1 ounce of sweet vermouth. If you like, you can add a dash of orange bitters to enhance the flavor profile.
3. Fill the mixing glass with ice cubes.
4. Using a bar spoon, gently stir the mixture for about 20–30 seconds.
5. If you chilled your glass with ice water, empty it now. Strain the stirred mixture into the chilled martini glass using a strainer.
6. Drop a maraschino cherry into the glass for a touch of color and additional sweetness.
7. Serve your Sweet Martini immediately, savoring its smooth and aromatic qualities.

Negroni Sbagliato Cocktail

The Negroni Sbagliato is a wonderful variation of the classic Negroni, offering a lighter and more festive option that's perfect for celebrations or casual gatherings. The word "sbagliato" means "mistaken" in Italian, and this drink was born from a happy accident where sparkling wine was used instead of gin. The result is a lighter, effervescent version of the Negroni, perfect for those who enjoy a bubbly twist.

PREP TIME: 5 Mins YIELD: 1 cocktail

GLASS

Traditionally served in an old-fashioned or rocks glass.

INGREDIENTS

* 1 oz (30 ml) sweet vermouth
* 1 oz (30 ml) Campari
* 1 oz (30 ml) Prosecco or other sparkling wine
* Ice cubes
* Orange slice or twist, for garnish

STEP-BY-STEP INSTRUCTIONS

1. Start by filling an old-fashioned glass with ice cubes to chill the drink.
2. Pour 1 ounce of Campari and 1 ounce of sweet vermouth directly into the glass over the ice.
3. Top the drink with 1 ounce of chilled Prosecco or your preferred sparkling wine. The bubbles add a delightful effervescence to the cocktail.
4. Gently stir the mixture with a bar spoon to combine the ingredients. Be careful not to stir too vigorously to maintain the bubbles from the sparkling wine.
5. Add a slice of orange or a twist of orange peel to the glass.
6. Serve your Negroni Sbagliato immediately.

Fear of Bravery

This cocktail is as sacred as its ingredients–a cocktail that portrays many flavors dancing without ever stepping on another's toes. What some might call a margarita variation, this refreshing, spicy, fruity, herbal blend of taste is best sipped: always.

INFO

PREP TIME:	15 min	GLASS ICE:	Cubes
SERVINGS:	24 cocktails	GARNISH:	Tajin Dipped Strawberry
GLASS:	Rocks Glass		
MIXING ICE:	Cubes		

MAKING THE DRINK

COCKTAIL-INGREDIENTS:

* Mezcal: 1 oz / 30 ml
* Yellow Chartreuse: 0.75 oz / 23 ml
* Blanc Vermouth: 0.5 oz / 15 ml
* Strawberry Jalapeño Syrup: 0.5 oz / 15 ml
* Lemon Juice: 0.75 oz / 23 ml

COCKTAIL-DIRECTIONS:

1. Add all ingredients to shaker tin.
2. Fill small tin with ice cubes.
3. Seal tin and shake for 5-6 seconds.
4. Strain into glass full of fresh ice.
5. Garnish with tajin dipped strawberry slice.

MAKING THE SYRUP

SYRUP-INGREDIENTS:

* Strawberries: 4 oz (weight) / 113g
* Jalapeño: 1 Jalapeño (deseeded)
* Sugar: 8 oz / 237 ml
* Water: 8 oz / 237 ml

PREP-DIRECTIONS:

1. Muddle strawberries and deseeded jalapeño into a pot before heating.
2. Add sugar and water, stir and muddle again within solution.
3. Add heat, stirring often until boiling, then turn off immediately.
4. Let sit for 5-10 minutes to infuse longer.
5. Strain and cool.

All That Jazz

The "Chet Baker" was coined by one of the most famous bars in NYC back in 2005. It spawned a domino effect of rum old fashioneds pouring out of drink wells around the world after that. This cocktail takes it back to the bourbon roots but with that same structure. Something to take the edge off and a lot of christmas in one glass...mug?

INFO

PREP TIME	20 min	MIXING ICE	Big Cube/ or Cubes
SERVINGS	56 cocktails	GLASS ICE	(same as mixing ice)
GLASS	Rocks Glass	GARNISH	Orange Peel

MAKING THE DRINK

COCKTAIL-INGREDIENTS:

* Bourbon: 2 oz / 60 ml
* Sweet Vermouth: 0.25 oz / 8 ml
* Cinnamon Honey: 1 Full Bar Spoon (0.2 oz / 6 ml)
Angostura Bitters: 1 Dash

COCKTAIL-DIRECTIONS:

1. Add all ingredients to a rocks glass.
2. Add big cube or multiple cubes.
3. Stir only 4-5 times.
4. Garnish with orange peel.

MAKING THE SYRUP

SYRUP-INGREDIENTS:

* Honey: 12 oz (weight) / 340g
* Water: 3 oz / 90ml
* Cinnamon Sticks: 1-2 Sticks or 0.5 tsp

PREP-DIRECTIONS:

1. Add honey and water to a pot and bring to a gentle simmer stirring constantly.
2. Once you see your first bubbles on the bottom of the pot turn off the heat and add cinnamon immediately and let sit for 5-10 minutes to soak.
3. Strain and cool.

Cheeky Smile

If you've never heard of a "Smash" it's exactly what it sounds like. You smash citrus and mint into alcohol and add a touch of sugar to balance it all out. Muddling the rind gives the cocktail more zing that just lemon juice and this allows even the strongest flavors to be tamed. In this variation of a Wry Grin, we brace for the smash before the fall flavors and then we prepare to pour them all over our lips.

Herbal, citrusy, bitter, refreshing.

INFO

PREP TIME: 15 min
SERVINGS: 16 cocktails
GLASS: Rocks Glass

MIXING ICE: Cubes
GLASS ICE: Cubes
GARNISH: Mint Sprig

MAKING THE DRINK

COCKTAIL-INGREDIENTS:

* Rye Whiskey: 1 oz / 30 ml
* Fernet Branca: 0.5 oz / 15 ml
* Dry Vermouth: 0.5 oz / 15 ml
* Apple Cider Syrup: 0.75 / 23 ml
* Lemon Slices: ⅜ of a Whole Lemon
* Mint: 6-8 Leaves

COCKTAIL-DIRECTIONS:

1. Add all ingredients into cocktail shaker.
2. Muddle lemon and mint into liquid.
3. Shake with ice for 7-8 seconds.
4. Strain into rocks glass with ice.
5. Crack ice on top to raise washline.
6. Garnish with a mint sprig.

MAKING THE SYRUP

SYRUP-INGREDIENTS:

* Apple Cider: 8 oz / 237 ml
* Sugar: 8 oz / 237 ml

PREP-DIRECTIONS:

1. Add apple cider and sugar to a pot.
2. Add heat stirring often until a boil or until sugar is dissolved.
3. Turn off heat and let cool.

Early Breakfast

The Irish Coffee is far from inclusive to the shires. Their steam broadcasts on sidewalks, bartops, porches, and window sills worldwide. The drink has very few ingredients but how those ingredients are combined make or break their construction. This version is the best we've ever tasted and incorporates our vermouth into the cream for a sweet savory kick.

INFO

PREP TIME: 15 min

SERVINGS:
SYRUP: 12 cocktails
CREAM: 3 cocktails

GLASS: Coffee Glass
MIXING ICE: None
GLASS ICE: None
GARNISH: Whip Cream / Coffee Salt

MAKING THE DRINK

COCKTAIL-INGREDIENTS:

* Irish Whiskey: 1.5 oz / 45 ml
* Coffee: 5 oz / 150 ml
* Demerara Syrup: 0.5 oz / 15 ml
* Sweet Vermouth Whip: 1.5 oz / 45 ml

COCKTAIL-DIRECTIONS:

1. Add demerara and whiskey to the glass.
2. Pour in hot coffee, leaving room for cream.
3. Whip your cream until thick, then float it on top of the coffee.
4. Add a pinch of coffee salt on top

MAKING THE SYRUP

SYRUP-INGREDIENTS:

* Demerara/Turbinado: 4 oz / 119 ml
* Water: 2 oz / 60 ml

PREP-DIRECTIONS:

1. Add dark sugar and water to a pot and stir before heating.
2. Add heat stirring constantly until it gently simmers (don't boil).
3. Simmer for 5 minutes or until sugar has fully dissolved and the solution looks smooth and clear.

MAKING THE CREAM VERMOUTH WHIPPED CREAM

WHIPPED CREAM INGREDIENTS:

* Heavy Cream: 4 oz / 119 ml
* Sweet Vermouth: .5 oz / 15 ml

WHIPPED CREAM DIRECTIONS:

1. Add heavy cream and sweet vermouth into a cocktail shaker.
2. Shake for 30-45 seconds or until thick, but not too thick.
3. Open the tin. It should be thick enough to slide out of the tin but not so thin that it pours quickly.

VERMOUTH WHIPPED CREAM (DAIRY-FREE)

OAT MILK WHIPPED CREAM INGREDIENTS:

* Oat Milk: 3 oz / 90 ml
* Coconut Oil: 1 oz / 30 ml
* Sweet Vermouth: 0.5 oz / 15 ml

OAT MILK WHIPPED CREAM DIRECTIONS:

1. Add oat milk, coconut oil and sweet vermouth into a cocktail shaker.
2. Shake for 30-45 seconds until thick.
3. Open the tin. It should be thick enough to slide out of the tin but no so thin that it moves quickly.

MAKING THE COFFEE SALT

COFFEE SALT INGREDIENTS:

* Coffee Grounds: 1 oz / 28.34 g
* Salt: 1 oz / 28.34 g

COFFEE SALT DIRECTIONS:

1. Add both to a small grinder
2. If already fine you can also mix them by hand.
3. Easy!

Vieux Carre

This classic needs no variation, though it is itself a variation of the Manhattan. This show stopper was created by Walter Bergeron at the Hotel Monteleone in New Orleans and is the drink people are proud to order when they think they know a little more than the average patron. Often made with high proof rye whiskey, and the split base of cognac gives it a complexity only our beautiful Sweet Vermouth can employ.

INFO

PREP TIME:	2 min	GLASS ICE:	(same as mixing ice)
SERVINGS:	Syrup: 1 cocktail	GARNISH:	Orange Peel w/ a Luxardo Cherry
GLASS:	Rocks Glass		
MIXING ICE:	Big Cube or Cubes		

MAKING THE DRINK

COCKTAIL-INGREDIENTS:

* Rye Whiskey: 1 oz / 30 ml
* Cognac: 1 oz / 30 ml
* Sweet Vermouth: 0.75 oz / 23 ml
* Benedictine: 0.25 oz / 8 ml
* Angostura Bitters: 1 Dash
* Peychaud's Bitters: 1 Dash

COCKTAIL-DIRECTIONS:

1. Add all ingredients to glass.
2. Add ice.
3. Stir 10-12 times or just enough for the glass to begin to feel cold.
4. Garnish with a Luxardo cherry wrapped inside an orange peel.

Quack Job

Scotch has always gotten a bad rap for its smokey flavors but then Mezcal and came and everybody hopped on board. Luckily, if drinking Scotch neat still isn't your preference, there are ingredients that not only balance but compliment the sharper flavors involved. This variation on the "Tattletale" is coaxes the honey and chocolate out of the Scotch by creating a stiff but delectable glass of dark flavors.

INFO

PREP TIME:	1 min	MIXING ICE:	Big Cubes or Cubes
SERVINGS:	1 cocktail	GLASS ICE:	(same as mixing ice)
GLASS:	Rocks Glass	GARNISH:	Orange Peel

MAKING THE DRINK

COCKTAIL-INGREDIENTS:

* Blended Scotch: 1.25 oz / 37 ml
* Islay Scotch: 0.75 oz / 23 ml
* Sweet Vermouth: 0.25 oz / 8 ml
* Averna: 0.25 oz / 8 ml
* Black Walnut Bitters: 2 Dashes

COCKTAIL-DIRECTIONS:

1. Add all ingredients to a rock glass.
2. Add ice to glass.
3. Stir only 4-5 times.
4. Garnish with and Orange Peel

Sherry Cobbler Special

Sherry and vermouth have much in common as they are both fortified wines. Vermouth though, is infused with herbs and botanicals giving it the complexity we all crave as a supporting role in classic drinks like the Manhattan and Martini. Balancing the boozy and herbal qualities with fruit and spice, the Cobbler family brings a holiday flavor profile that warms our heart even on the coldest of evenings.

INFO

PREP TIME	15 min	GLASS ICE	Crushed
SERVINGS	12 cocktails	GARNISH	Orange Peel + Berries
GLASS	Rocks Glass		
MIXING ICE	2 Cubes		

MAKING THE DRINK

COCKTAIL-INGREDIENTS:

* Amontillado Sherry: 1 oz / 30 ml
* Sweet Vermouth: 1 oz / 30 ml
* Cinnamon Syrup: 0.5 oz / 15 ml
* Lemon Juice: 0.75oz / 23ml
* Assorted Berries: 3 berries total

COCKTAIL-DIRECTIONS:

1. Add all ingredients into small tin.
2. Muddle berries.
3. Fill small tin with 2 ice cubes and shake for 4-5 seconds.
4. Dump everything into rocks glass.
5. Add crushed ice.
6. Garnish with an orange peel and berries.

MAKING THE SYRUP

SYRUP-INGREDIENTS:

* Sugar: 4 oz / 119ml
* Water: 4 oz / 119ml
* Cinnamon Sticks: 1-1.5 Sticks or 0.75 tsp

PREP-DIRECTIONS:

1. Add all ingredients to a pot.
2. Stir sugar and water before heating.
3. Heat to a simmer, let simmer for 5-10 minutes.
4. Strain and cool.

Florence Flowers

Notorious for heating us up, alcohol actually does a great job of refreshing us on a hot day. The "spritz" cocktail family came into the scene strong and is now one of the most popular drinks you can order. Variations have come and gone but one thing is for sure: people want it light and with refreshing ingredients. This take on the Hugo Spritz shows how Blanc Vermouth can be a versatile summer asset.

INFO

PREP TIME	2 min	MIXING ICE	Cubes
SERVINGS	1 cocktail	GLASS ICE	(same as mixing ice)
GLASS	White Wine Glass	GARNISH	Mint Sprig

MAKING THE DRINK

COCKTAIL-INGREDIENTS:

* Blanc Vermouth: 1 oz / 30 ml
* Elderflower Liqueur: 1 oz / 30 ml
* Sparkling Wine: 3 oz / 90 ml
* Soda: 1 oz / 30 ml
* Muddled Mint: 4-6 Leaves

COCKTAIL-DIRECTIONS:

1. Add all liquids to glass.
2. Muddle mint.
3. Fill with ice cubes.
4. Quick stir.
5. Garnish with mint sprig.

Vineyard Sting

The Bee's Knees is not only a saying from the 1920's, it's a cocktail that dates back to that era as well. Originally this gin sour with a touch of honey had the ambition to hide the taste of poorly made gin during prohibition, but today, it is a staple of the ability to use a trilogy of ingredients to balance any cocktail. This variation incorporates many bartenders' favorite additions to that classic, while showing that the base spirit can be replaced seamlessly. Here we exemplify how low-abv cocktails find their inspirations. Tangy, refreshing, and a whole lot of zing.

INFO

PREP TIME	15 min	MIXING ICE	Cubes
SERVINGS	16 cocktails	GLASS ICE	None (served up)
GLASS	Coupe Glass	GARNISH	Grapefruit Twist

MAKING THE DRINK

COCKTAIL-INGREDIENTS:

* White Wine: 1 oz / 30 ml
* Dry Vermouth: 1 oz / 30 ml
* Regal Honey Syrup: 0.75 oz / 23 ml
* Lemon Juice: 0.75oz / 23ml
* Angostura Bitters: 2 Dashes

COCKTAIL-DIRECTIONS:

1. Add all ingredients to small tin.
2. Fill small tin with ice and shake for 8-9 seconds or until tin is properly chilled.
3. Strain into coupe glass.
4. Garnish with small grapefruit twist

MAKING THE SYRUP

SYRUP-INGREDIENTS:

* Honey: 12 oz (weight) / 8.1 oz volume / 240 ml
* Water: 3 oz / 89 ml
* Grapefruit Peels: 2-3 peels

PREP-DIRECTIONS:

1. Add honey and water to a pot.
2. Stirring constantly, bring to simmer.
3. Turn off heat once bubbles show.
4. Add 2-3 pithless grapefruit peels once the liquid has cooled but is still hot (around 140F) and let sit for 5-10 minutes.
5. Strain and cool.

So Soon

By now you may see that split base cocktails are common. As long as you account for the balance of alcohol, sweetness, and acid, you can split any ingredient up to make room for more. The Too Soon is an amazing example of how splitting your base with an Amaro (Italian bitter liqueur) can add depth to any cocktail. Here we use Cynar which is an Artichoke leaf infused Amaro. Sounds crazier than it tastes–once mixed with these ingredients.

INFO

PREP TIME	15 min	MIXING ICE	Cubes
SERVINGS	12 cocktails	GLASS ICE	None (served up)
GLASS	Coupe Glass	GARNISH	Orange Peel

MAKING THE DRINK

COCKTAIL-INGREDIENTS:

* Gin: 1 oz / 30 ml
* Cynar: 0.5 oz / 15 ml
* Sweet Vermouth: 0.5 oz / 15 ml
* Cinnamon Syrup: 0.5 oz / 15 ml
* Lemon Juice: 0.75oz / 23ml
* Orange Slice: 1 Muddled Slice

COCKTAIL-DIRECTIONS:

1. Add all liquids to small tin.
2. Muddled orange slice in liquid.
3. Fill small tin with ice and shake for 8-9 seconds or until tin is properly cold.
4. Strain into coupe glass.
5. Garnish with orange twist

MAKING THE SYRUP

SYRUP-INGREDIENTS:

* Sugar: 4 oz / 119ml
* Water: 4 oz / 119ml
* Cinnamon Sticks: 1-1.5 Sticks / 0.75 tsp Ground

PREP-DIRECTIONS:

1. Add sugar and water to a pot and stir.
2. Add cinnamon and begin heating.
3. Heat to a simmer, and let simmer for 5-10 minutes.
4. Strain and cool.

Arch-Nemesis

May we not forget that sometimes we want a stronger drink to take the edge off. This doesn't mean we have to take shots and it doesn't mean we have to sacrifice flavor. Martini's are an excellent base to tweak and make our own, especially when wanting to incorporate vermouth. This variation on the Archangel cocktail goes slightly lower-abv without smothering the booze in citrus. Martini style, but a whole lot more palatable throughout the night.

INFO

PREP TIME	15 min	MIXING ICE	Cubes
SERVINGS	30 cocktails	GLASS ICE	None (served up)
GLASS	Coupe Glass	GARNISH	Cucumber Slice

MAKING THE DRINK

COCKTAIL-INGREDIENTS:

* Gin: 1.5 oz / 45 ml
* Dry Vermouth: 0.75 oz / 23 ml
* Aperol: 0.75 oz / 23 ml
* Raspberry Syrup: 1 Bar Spoon
* Cucumber Slices 2 Slices

COCKTAIL-DIRECTIONS:

1. Add all liquids to mixing glass.
2. Muddle 2 cucumbers slices into it.
3. Fill with ice and mix for a minute or until mixing glass becomes cold.
4. Strain into glass.
5. Garnish with cucumber slice and raspberry.

MAKING THE SYRUP

SYRUP-INGREDIENTS:

* Sugar: 4 oz / 119ml
* Water: 2 oz / 60ml
* Raspberries: 10 Berries

PREP-DIRECTIONS:

1. Add all ingredients to a pot.
2. Muddle raspberries.
3. Add heat, stirring often, until.a simmer and let simmer for 5-10 minutes.
4. Remove from heat.
5. Strain and cool.

Pluto

Tiki drinks shall not be ignored in this book, because vermouth is not only for Martinis. The Saturn is a cocktail that proved the same for Gin, making it an absolute favorite behind walls of masks and tiki torches. Using Dry Vermouth as our base we can compliment the unique botanicals with fruity tropical delicacies, and yes, it will look pretty too!

INFO

PREP TIME	15 min	MIXING ICE	2 Cubes
SERVINGS	20 cocktails	GLASS ICE	Crushed
GLASS	Coupe Glass	GARNISH	Flower

MAKING THE DRINK

COCKTAIL-INGREDIENTS:

* Dry Vermouth: 1.5 oz / 45 ml
* Falernum: 0.5 oz / 15 ml
* Passionfruit Juice: 0.5 oz / 15 ml
* Acai Orgeat: 0.5 oz / 15ml
* Lemon Juice: 0.75oz / 23ml

COCKTAIL-DIRECTIONS:

1. Add all ingredients to small tin.
2. Fill with ice.
3. Shake for 8-9 seconds or until tin feels properly cold.
4. Strain into coupe glass.
5. Garnish with a flower.

MAKING THE SYRUP

SYRUP-INGREDIENTS:

* Almond Milk: 7 oz / 208 ml
* Sugar: 16 oz / 475 ml
* Acai (frozen or juice): 1 oz / 30 ml
* Almond Extract: .5 Tsp
* Orange Flower Water: 1 Tsp

PREP-DIRECTIONS:

1. Blend all ingredients until incorporated.
2. Strain.

White Negroni

Surely you've heard of a Negroni and if you haven't that's ok. It's a cocktail that breaks the norm and has an equal part recipe of spirit, amaro, and vermouth. As alcohols developed more variety, so too did the cocktails we could make. The gentian liqueurs like Campari could be substituted for others that were clear like Salers or Suze and Blanc Vermouth became a bartender's best friend on hot days on in lighter drinks. This boozy combination gives you something that becomes greater than the sum of its parts. A strong but smooth drink with a bite.

INFO

PREP TIME	2 min	MIXING ICE	Big Cube or Cubes
SERVINGS	1 cocktail	GLASS ICE	(same as mixing ice)
GLASS	Rocks Glass	GARNISH	Lemon Peel

MAKING THE DRINK

COCKTAIL-INGREDIENTS:

* Gin: 1 oz / 30 ml
* Blanc Vermouth: 1 oz / 30 ml
* Salers or Suze (or other clear gentian liqueur): 1 oz / 30 ml

COCKTAIL-DIRECTIONS:

1. Add all ingredients to rocks glass.
2. Add big cube or multiple cubes.
3. Quick stir, 8-10 times revolutions.
4. Garnish with a lemon peel.

Dram-Com

The Romantic Comedy cocktail took the bar scene by storm. We all want a pink drink that still packs a punch and Aperol has won its right to sit on every shelf. This vermouth version has all the things that make a great cocktail, refreshing, citrusy, tangy, slightly bitter complexity, and herbal with cucumber to lighten the load. It's so well balanced that the summer olympics wishes they had gymnastics too.

INFO

PREP TIME	2 min	MIXING ICE	Cubes
SERVINGS	12 cocktails	GLASS ICE	Cubes
GLASS	Rocks Glass	GARNISH	Cucumber Slice

MAKING THE DRINK

COCKTAIL-INGREDIENTS:

* Blanc Vermouth: 1.5 oz / 45 ml
* Aperol: 1 oz / 30 ml
* Simple Syrup: 0.25 oz / 8 ml
* Cucumber Juice: 0.5 oz / 15 ml
* Lemon Juice: 0.75oz / 23 ml

COCKTAIL-DIRECTIONS:

1. Add all ingredients into small tin.
2. Add ice and shake for 4-5 seconds.
3. Strain into rocks glass with fresh ice.
4. Garnish with Cucumber Slice

MAKING THE SYRUP

Simple Syrup:

SYRUP-INGREDIENTS:

* Sugar: 4 oz / 119ml
* Water: 4 oz / 119ml

PREP-DIRECTIONS:

1. Add all ingredients to a pot.
2. Stir sugar and water before heating.
3. Stir until a boil.
4. Strain and cool.

Bijou

We've spoken about trilogies in refreshing cocktails but there is a magic formula in Martini's too. The Bijou was said to represent the three jewels, Gin as the diamond, Green Chartreuse and the emerald, and Sweet Vermouth as the ruby. This drink is elegant and sips like royalty as well. Herbal, rich, but kicks like a stallion.

INFO

PREP TIME	2 min	MIXING ICE	Cubes
SERVINGS	1 cocktail	GLASS ICE	None (served up)
GLASS	Coupe Glass	GARNISH	Orange Peel

MAKING THE DRINK

COCKTAIL-INGREDIENTS:

* Gin: 1.5 oz / 45 ml
* Green Chartreuse: 0.75 oz / 23 ml
* Sweet Vermouth: 0.75 oz / 23 ml
* Orange Bitters: 2 Dashes

COCKTAIL-DIRECTIONS:

1. Add all ingredients to mixing glass.
2. Fill with ice and stir for a minute or until mixing glass is chilled.
3. Strain into coupe glass.
4. Garnish with an orange twist.

Americano Zest

If you order an Americano, most people think you'll get a shot of espresso and hot water in a glass. At a bar you must be more careful, because a delicious, lighter, low-abv Negroni riff may surprise your table. This equal parts cocktail is an easy sipper but still low acid.

INFO

PREP TIME	2 min	MIXING ICE	Cubes
SERVINGS	1 cocktail	GLASS ICE	(Same as mixing ice)
GLASS	Collins Glass	GARNISH	Orange Peel

MAKING THE DRINK

COCKTAIL-INGREDIENTS:

* Campari: 1.5 oz / 45 ml
* Sweet Vermouth: 1.5 oz / 45 ml
* Grapefruit Soda: 2-3 oz / 60-90 ml

COCKTAIL-DIRECTIONS:

1. Add all campari and sweet vermouth to a collins glass.
2. Fill with ice.
3. Top with grapefruit soda.
4. Garnish with an orange peel.

Monte Bianco

This take on the classic Cobble Hill take a lightened manhattan variation a step further with gin as the horse and a Blanc Vermouth and Montenegro holding the reins. Floral and viscous, stiff and luscious.

INFO

PREP TIME	< 1 minute	MIXING ICE	Cubes
SERVINGS	1 cocktail	GLASS ICE	None (Served Up)
GLASS	Coupe Glass	GARNISH	Lemon Twist

MAKING THE DRINK

COCKTAIL-INGREDIENTS:

* Chamomile Gin: 2 oz / 60 ml
* Bianco Vermouth: 0.5 oz / 15 ml
* Amaro Montengro: 0.5 oz / 15 ml
* Bruised Cucumber Slices: 2 Slices

COCKTAIL-DIRECTIONS:

1. Add all ingredients to mixing glass.
2. Muddle cucumber.
3. Fill the mixing glass with ice.
4. Stir for 30 seconds or until mixing glass is cold.
5. Strain.
6. Garnish.

Venice Heatwave

This drink is a tropical breeze with tangy but fruity flavors and aromas. It sips quickly and is a variation on the East 8 Hold Up, a fan favorite around the world. To try the original, replace mango puree with passionfruit to see what started all this fuss.

INFO

PREP TIME	20 min	MIXING ICE	2 Cubes
SERVINGS	18 cocktails	GLASS ICE	Crushed
GLASS	Collins/Tiki Glass	GARNISH	Mint Sprig

MAKING THE DRINK

COCKTAIL-INGREDIENTS:

* Rum: 1.5oz / 45 ml
* Banana Syrup: .5 oz / 15 ml
* Pineapple: 1 oz / 30 ml
* Lemon: .5 oz / 15 ml
* Sweet Vermouth: .25 oz / 8ml

COCKTAIL-DIRECTIONS:

1. Add all ingredients to shaker tin except vermouth.
2. Add 2 ice cubes.
3. Shake for 2-3 seconds.
4. Dump whole drink and ice into glass.
5. Top with crushed ice.
6. Float 0.25 oz / 8ml of vermouth on top.
7. Garnish with mint sprig.

MAKING THE SYRUP

SYRUP-INGREDIENTS:

* Bananas: 1 Large Banana
* Sugar: 8 oz / 237 ml
* Water: 4 oz / 119 ml

PREP-DIRECTIONS:

1. Mix sugar and water into a pot.
2. Add and muddle bananas into solution.
3. Add heat and stir often until you reach a boil.
4. Strain (Let bananas sit longer for a stronger flavor).

Disappearing Act

This one slips away like a winter sunset but is best consumed in summer. A variation on the classic "Hole in the Cup" you'll soon see where it got its name. Refreshing and citrus forward, this cool tangy blast is frothy and herbaceous.

INFO

PREP TIME	15 min	MIXING ICE	Cubes
SERVINGS	16 cocktails	GLASS ICE	None (Served Up)
GLASS	Coupe Glass	GARNISH	Cucumber Slice

MAKING THE DRINK

COCKTAIL-INGREDIENTS

* Tequila: 1.5oz / 45 ml
* Dry Vermouth: 0.5 oz / 15 ml
* Cucumber Syrup: 0.5 oz / 15 ml
* Pineapple Juice: 1 oz / 30 ml
* Lemon Juice: .5 oz / 15 ml
* Absinthe: Spray/Rinse

COCKTAIL-DIRECTIONS

1. Spray or rinse absinthe in coupe glass.
2. Add all ingredients to small shaker tin.
3. Fill small tin with ice cubes.
4. Seal tins and shake for 9-10 seconds.
5. Strain into glass.
6. Garnish for cucumber slice.

MAKING THE SYRUP

SYRUP-INGREDIENTS

* Cucumber Juice: 8 oz / 237 ml
* Sugar: 8 oz / 237 ml

PREP-DIRECTIONS

1. Juice 1 cucumbers and strain
2. Add all ingredients to blender and blend until sugar is fully dissolved.
3. Strain solution.

Adonis Cocktail

The Adonis cocktail is a classic yet somewhat underappreciated drink that dates back to the late 19th century. Named after a Broadway musical of the same era, this cocktail is known for its smooth, sherry-forward profile with a touch of sweetness from the vermouth.

PREP TIME 5 Mins

YIELD 1 cocktail

GLASS

Traditionally served in a chilled coupe or cocktail glass.

INGREDIENTS

* 1 1/2 oz (45 ml) dry sherry
* 1 1/2 oz (45 ml) sweet vermouth
* 2 dashes of orange bitters
* Ice cubes
* Orange twist or lemon twist, for garnish

STEP-BY-STEP INSTRUCTIONS

1. Begin by chilling your coupe or cocktail glass. You can do this by placing it in the freezer for a few minutes or filling it with ice water while you prepare the cocktail.
2. In a mixing glass, combine 1 1/2 ounces of dry sherry and 1 1/2 ounces of sweet vermouth.
3. Add two dashes of orange bitters to the mixing glass. Then, fill the mixing glass with ice cubes to chill the mixture.
4. Using a bar spoon, stir the mixture gently for about 20–30 seconds. This helps to chill and slightly dilute the cocktail, enhancing the balance of flavors.
5. If you chilled your glass with ice water, empty it now. Strain the stirred mixture into the chilled coupe or cocktail glass using a strainer.
6. For a garnish, twist a strip of orange or lemon peel over the drink to release its aromatic oils, and then drop it into the glass.
7. Serve your Adonis cocktail immediately, savoring its light, aromatic, and slightly sweet profile.

Martinez Cocktail

The Martinez cocktail is a classic drink, often considered the precursor to the modern Martini. It is a delightful blend of gin and sweet vermouth, with a touch of maraschino liqueur and bitters, offering a complex and aromatic profile. This cocktail is perfect for those who appreciate a slightly sweeter and more flavorful gin-based drink.

PREP TIME 5 Mins   YIELD 1 COCKTAIL

GLASS

Traditionally served in a chilled martini glass.

INGREDIENTS

* 1/2 oz (45 ml) gin
* 1 1/2 oz (45 ml) sweet vermouth
* 1/4 oz (7.5 ml) maraschino liqueur
* 2 dashes of orange bitters
* Ice cubes
* Lemon twist, for garnish

STEP-BY-STEP INSTRUCTIONS

1. Begin by chilling your coupe or martini glass. Place it in the freezer for a few minutes or fill it with ice water while you prepare the cocktail.
2. In a mixing glass, combine 1 1/2 ounces of gin, 1 1/2 ounces of sweet vermouth, and 1/4 ounce of maraschino liqueur.
3. Add two dashes of orange bitters to the mixing glass. Fill the mixing glass with ice cubes to chill the mixture.
4. Using a bar spoon, stir the cocktail gently for about 20–30 seconds.
5. If you used ice water to chill your glass, empty it now. Strain the stirred mixture into the chilled coupe or martini glass using a strainer.
6. Twist a strip of lemon peel over the drink to release its aromatic oils, then drop it into the glass as a garnish.
7. Serve your Martinez cocktail immediately, enjoying its rich and aromatic complexity.

Vermouth Cassis Cocktail

The Vermouth Cassis is a refreshing and fruity cocktail that combines the aromatic qualities of vermouth with the rich, sweet flavors of crème de cassis, a blackcurrant liqueur. It's ideal as an aperitif or a light, flavorful drink for any occasion.

PREP TIME 5 Mins YIELD 1 cocktail

GLASS

Traditionally served in a chilled rocks or old-fashioned glass.

INGREDIENTS

* 2 oz (60 ml) dry vermouth
* 1 oz (30 ml) crème de cassis
* Club soda or sparkling water, to top
* Ice cubes
* Lemon slice or twist, for garnish

STEP-BY-STEP INSTRUCTIONS

1. Begin by filling a rocks or old-fashioned glass with ice cubes to chill the drink.
2. Pour 2 ounces of dry vermouth and 1 ounce of crème de cassis over the ice in the glass.
3. Add a splash of club soda or sparkling water to the glass to give the cocktail a refreshing effervescence. Adjust the amount based on your preference for strength and fizz.
4. Gently stir the mixture with a bar spoon to combine the ingredients and chill the cocktail evenly.
5. Add a lemon slice or a twist of lemon peel for a touch of citrus aroma that complements the flavors of the drink.
6. Serve your Vermouth Cassis immediately, enjoying its refreshing and fruity profile.

Vermouth Cobbler Cocktail

The Vermouth Cobbler is a delightful and easy-to-make cocktail with a base of vermouth, which is sweetened and enhanced by fresh fruit and a touch of sugar. It's served over crushed ice, making it not only delicious but also quite attractive.

PREP TIME 10 Mins YIELD 1 cocktail

GLASS

Traditionally served in a cobbler or large wine glass.

INGREDIENTS

* 3 oz (90 ml) sweet vermouth
* 1 teaspoon sugar (optional, adjust based on sweetness preference)
* Assorted fresh fruits, diced (such as orange, apple, kiwi, berries, and cherries)
* Crushed ice
* Mint sprig, for garnish

STEP-BY-STEP INSTRUCTIONS

1. Fill a cobbler or large wine glass with crushed ice, packing it tightly to chill the glass.
2. Pour 3 ounces of sweet vermouth over the crushed ice in the glass.
3. If desired, add a teaspoon of sugar. This step is optional and can be adjusted based on your sweetness preference.
4. Stir gently to help the sugar dissolve.
5. Garnish the drink with a variety of fresh fruits. You can add slices of orange, diced apple or kiwi, a handful of berries, and a maraschino cherry for both flavor and visual appeal.
6. Finish with a sprig of fresh mint to add a refreshing aroma to the cocktail.
7. Serve your Vermouth Cobbler immediately with a straw or a spoon to enjoy the refreshing mix of flavors and textures.

Vermouth Diplomat Cream

PREP TIME	20 mins	RESTING TIME	5 hours
COOK TIME	10 mins	SERVINGS	6-8

INGREDIENTS

* 2 cups (500 ml) whole milk
* 1/2 cup (100 g) granulated sugar
* 4 egg yolks
* 1/4 cup (30 g) cornstarch
* 1 teaspoon vanilla extract
* 2 tablespoons (30 ml) sweet vermouth
* 1 cup (240 ml) heavy cream
* 2 tablespoons (25 g) powdered sugar

STEP-BY-STEP INSTRUCTIONS

MAKE THE PASTRY CREAM:

1. In a medium saucepan, heat the milk over medium heat until it's just about to boil. Remove from heat and set aside.
2. In a mixing bowl, whisk together the egg yolks and granulated sugar until the mixture is pale and creamy.
3. Whisk the cornstarch into the egg mixture until smooth and fully combined.
4. Gradually add the hot milk to the egg mixture, whisking constantly to prevent the eggs from curdling.
5. Return the mixture to the saucepan and cook over medium heat, stirring constantly, until it thickens and starts to bubble. This should take about 5–7 minutes.
6. Remove from heat and stir in the vanilla extract and vermouth. Mix until well combined.
7. Pour the pastry cream into a bowl, cover it with plastic wrap touching the surface to prevent a skin from forming, and let it cool to room temperature. Then refrigerate until fully chilled.

MAKE THE WHIPPED CREAM:

1. In a large mixing bowl, beat the heavy cream with an electric mixer on medium speed until it starts to thicken.
2. Gradually add the powdered sugar and continue beating until soft peaks form.

COMBINE:

1. Once the pastry cream is chilled, gently fold the whipped cream into the pastry cream using a spatula. Mix until fully combined and smooth.
2. Chill the Diplomat Cream for at least an hour in the refrigerator to let the flavors meld together.
3. Serve it in individual dessert cups, or use it as a filling for pastries and cakes.

Vermouth-Poached Pears

The Vermouth-Poached Pears are an elegant dessert option, offering a delightful balance of sweetness and spice, with the vermouth adding a distinct aromatic flavor. Perfect for a dinner party or a special treat!

PREP TIME 10 min
COOK TIME 40 mins
SERVINGS 4

INGREDIENTS

* 4 ripe but firm pears (such as Bosc or Anjou), peeled, with stems intact
* 2 cups sweet vermouth
* 1 cup water
* 1/2 cup sugar
* 1 cinnamon stick
* 3-4 whole cloves
* 1 vanilla bean, split lengthwise (or 1 teaspoon vanilla extract)
* Zest of 1 lemon (optional)

STEP-BY-STEP INSTRUCTIONS

1. In a large saucepan, combine the vermouth, water, sugar, cinnamon stick, cloves, vanilla bean, and lemon zest. Bring the mixture to a simmer over medium heat, stirring occasionally, until the sugar has dissolved.
2. Place the peeled pears into the poaching liquid. If necessary, add more water to ensure the pears are submerged.
3. Reduce the heat to low and cover the saucepan with a lid. Let the pears simmer gently for about 20–30 minutes, or until they are tender when pierced with a knife. Turn the pears occasionally to ensure even cooking.
4. Once cooked, remove the pears from the liquid and set them aside to cool slightly. Increase the heat and bring the poaching liquid to a boil. Allow it to reduce until it becomes a syrupy consistency, about 10–15 minutes.
5. Serve the pears warm or at room temperature, drizzled with the reduced vermouth syrup.

5
A Quiet Icon of Style

Vermouth might not always take center stage, but in the world of cinema and television, it's often the unsung hero of sophistication. Whether swirled into a crisp martini or stirred into a smoky Manhattan, vermouth shows up in the hands of spies, romantics, mobsters, and aesthetes — a subtle symbol of taste, control, and culture.

Its presence is rarely loud, but it speaks volumes. A splash of dry vermouth in a Bond martini tells us the drinker is exacting and cool under pressure. A bottle of sweet vermouth behind a 1960s Madison Avenue bar cart in *Mad Men* signals elegance and emotional armor. In noir films, classic dramas, and even animated kitchens, vermouth adds depth — not just to cocktails, but to character.

It's the drink of people who know what they want, or at least pretend to. In that way, vermouth is more than a mixer — it's a mood.

James Bond - Dr. No

Vermouth Moment: Bond orders a classic dry vodka martini, "shaken, not stirred."

This is the film where James Bond's iconic cocktail first hits the screen — dry vermouth quietly plays its part, signaling Bond's refined taste and deadly precision. The drink becomes a character trait in itself.

Mad Men

Vermouth Moment: Don Draper and colleagues regularly drink Manhattans, Martinis, and other vermouth-heavy classics.

Vermouth is practically part of the office furniture at Sterling Cooper. It's a quiet but constant presence, mixed into drinks that reflect power, stress, charm — and a longing to escape it all.

Casablanca

Vermouth Moment: A patron orders a Vermouth Cassis, a classic French apéritif.

Amid the smoke and shadows of Rick's Café, this bittersweet drink evokes a lost European elegance. It's a subtle nod to memory, nostalgia, and everything the war-torn characters have left behind.

Ingrid
Paul
BOGART
HENREI
Casablanca
CLAUDE RAINS
SIDNEY GREENSTREET

All About Eve

Vermouth Moment: A classic Martini is sipped at a stylish party.

In a world of biting dialogue and sharp ambition, the martini — and the dry vermouth in it — serves as a social weapon, signaling sophistication and control among Broadway's elite.

James Bond - Skyfall

Vermouth Moment: The Vesper Martini is updated; Bond drinks at a luxury casino bar.

More than just a throwback, vermouth in *Skyfall* represents Bond's continuity — a throughline from Connery to Craig. The cocktail, like Bond himself, evolves but never loses its cool.

6
Vermouth Culture Today

If you think Vermouth is just a relic from dusty cocktail books or old-school Italian cafés, think again. Vermouth is having a serious moment—and it's thriving in places far beyond the back bar. From neighborhood vermuterías to sleek, modern cocktail temples, Vermouth is being rediscovered by a new generation of drinkers who are embracing its versatility and charm.

The Return of the Aperitif Hour

In Italy and Spain, the aperitif never really went out of style. But today, the culture around Vermouth—*la hora del vermut* in Spain or *l'ora dell'aperitivo* in Italy—is being revived with fresh enthusiasm.

In cities like Madrid, Barcelona, Milan, and Turin, people are reclaiming that magical window of time between work and dinner. The vibe is casual yet intentional: Vermouth served over ice with a slice of orange or a green olive, paired with small bites like marinated anchovies, potato chips, or almonds. No rush, no fuss—just good company and a glass that invites conversation.

Even outside of southern Europe, this "slow drinking" ritual is catching on. In New York, London, and Melbourne, bars are offering early evening menus dedicated to low-ABV aperitifs and light snacks, reviving a culture of savoring, not just sipping.

Vermouth Bars & Vermuterías

Step into a vermutería, and you'll feel the pulse of modern Vermouth culture. These bars, especially popular in Spain and now cropping up worldwide, center around one thing: Vermouth as the star.

In Barcelona, tiny spots with tiled walls and handwritten menus serve house Vermut on tap, usually red and slightly sweet, poured over ice and garnished with citrus or olive. Patrons crowd in for the social aspect as much as the drink itself—*vermouth time* is about togetherness.

In Paris, vermouth-focused bars offer curated lists of French and Italian labels, served alongside oysters, pâté, and crusty baguettes.

Stateside, spots like Brooklyn's "Sunset Vermouth Hour" pop-ups and San Francisco's vermouth flights are part of a wider trend of rediscovery. Whether poured straight, spritzed with soda, or stirred into cocktails, Vermouth is front and center.

The Craft Vermouth Movement

One major reason Vermouth feels fresh again is the rise of artisanal producers who are bringing creativity and care to every bottle.

Bartenders, winemakers, and distillers are collaborating to experiment with native botanicals, alternative wine bases, and sustainable production methods. In California, you'll find Vermouths made with local Pinot Noir or Vermentino grapes. In Australia, producers like Maidenii are playing with bush tomatoes and wattleseed. Even in the UK and Scandina-

VERMUTERÍA
LA ROSA
Chica
CASA DE COMIDAS

via, modern makers are adding local twists—seaweed, heather, Nordic berries, and more.

The craft movement has shifted Vermouth from being just a cocktail component to a sippable, standalone star. These Vermouths are often made in small batches with organic ingredients, appealing to drinkers who care about provenance and flavor nuance.

Vermouth's Role in Modern Cocktails

The global cocktail scene has also been pivotal in Vermouth's renaissance. Bartenders are leaning into its versatility—not just as a supporting actor, but as a lead.

* **Low-ABV Cocktails:** With wellness and moderation top of mind, low-alcohol cocktails like Vermouth spritzes, Americano riffs, or simple Vermouth-and-tonic drinks are taking over menus.

* **Modern Classics:** Vermouth is showing up in reimagined versions of classics. Bartenders are swapping sweet Vermouths for bianco or aged versions, adding a twist to drinks like the Negroni or Manhattan.

* **House-Made Vermouth:** Some cocktail bars are even crafting their own bespoke Vermouth blends, dialing in botanical profiles to suit their seasonal menus or house styles. This hands-on approach makes Vermouth feel personal and special—tailored to the drinker's experience.

The Culture of Savoring

In a world often defined by speed and instant gratification, Vermouth culture today is a subtle rebellion. It invites you to slow down, sip thoughtfully, and engage in conversation.

This isn't just about drinking—it's about the mood Vermouth sets:

* Lingering longer at the table.
* Swapping stories at a sunlit bar.
* Watching the city go by with a cool glass in hand.

Whether you're in a bustling vermutería in Barcelona or making a quiet spritz at home, Vermouth connects you to a tradition that's both timeless and totally of the moment.

A Global Aperitif, Forever Evolving

Today's Vermouth landscape is vibrant and diverse. There are still the venerable houses—Carpano, Noilly Prat, Dolin—anchoring the category. But alongside them, there's a new wave of adventurous producers and enthusiastic drinkers rediscovering what Vermouth can be.

It's no longer just something you dash into a cocktail. It's something to explore on its own terms. Sipped slowly, shared widely.

The best part? We're still just at the beginning of this new chapter in Vermouth's story.

PHOTO CREDITS
4: nnattalli / shutterstock.com
7: page frederique / Shutterstock.com
8-9: Everett Collection / shutterstock.com
11: Maksym Fesenko / Shutterstock
12: Lukasz Szwaj / Shutterstock.com
15: Heike Rau - Shutterstock.com
16-17: Shchipkova Elena / Shutterstock.com
20-21: siamionau pavel / Shutterstock.com
22: Luigi Bertello / Shutterstock.com
25: Cyrille LIPS / Shutterstock.com
26-27: Artesia Wells / Shutterstock.com
31: KarenHBlack / Shutterstock.com
32: REPORT / Shutterstock.com
34: Fanta Media / Shutterstock.com
35: barinart / Shutterstock.com
36-37: Nicolas ezequiel Marquez / Shutterstock.com
38: Pierre-Olivier / shutterstock.com
39: Irik Bik / Shutterstock.com
40: SkazovD / Shutterstock.com
Drink photos: Sean Ryan
110: pausestudio / Shutterstock.com
113: Collection Christophel / Alamy Stock Photo
114: PictureLux / The Hollywood Archive / Alamy Stock Photo
117: spatuletail / Shutterstock.com
118: Allstar Picture Library Limited / Alamy Stock Photo
121: landmarkmedia / Shutterstock.com
122-123: 5PH / Shutterstock.com
124: Ryzhkov Photography / Shutterstock.com
126-127: Deliris / Shutterstock.com
129: Artesia Wells / Shutterstock.com
130: Miguel Tamayo Fotografia / Shutterstock.com
134-135: 5PH / Shutterstock.com

Vermouth – A Classic Revival

Text: Sean Ryan & Jesper Helmin
Editor: Jesper Helmin
Layout: Anders Gerning

ISBN: 978-87-94190-93-0
1. edition, 1. circulation
Printed at PrintBest, Estonia, 2026

Helmin Publishing
Nivå Strandpark 21
DK-2990 Nivå
Denmark

www.helminpublishing.dk